Over and Out

John Townsend

SEN Department
St. Benedict's Senior School
54 Eaton Rise
Ealing
LONDON W5 2ES
020 8862 2000

Stanley Thornes (Publishers) Ltd

Contents

First published 1988 by Hutchinson Education

Reprinted 1991 by
Stanley Thornes (Publishers) Ltd
Ellenborough House
Wellington Street
CHELTENHAM GL50 1YW
England

99 00 01 02 03 / 10 9 8 7 6

British Library Cataloguing in Publication Data

Townsend, John, 1924–
    Over and out.—(Spirals).
    1. English language – Readers – For slow
learning students
    I. Title   II. Series
    428.6'2

    ISBN 0 7487 1002 7

Cover illustration by Simon Rees
Cover design by Ned Hoste
Printed and bound in Great Britain by Martin's The Printers, Berwick

All Fingers and Thumbs

2 parts:
Fingers (a bank robber with a walkie-talkie), P.C. Thumbs
(a police officer with a radio). Radio noises made by both!

Fingers	Oi! Are you there?
Radio	Buzz . . . gurgle . . . splutter.
Fingers	Come in, over.
Radio	Splutter . . . gurgle . . . buzz.
Fingers	Oi! Do you read me?
Radio	Click . . . rumble . . . hummmmm.
Fingers	I bet he's not tuned in or turned on.
Radio	Brrrr . . . hic . . . hic . . . grrrrr . . . zzzzzzzzzzzz.
Fingers	It makes me sick. Here I am taking all the risks and he can't even do his part of the job. Oi! Do you read me?
Radio	Plunk . . . gurgle . . . gurgle . . . sp sp sp sp . . . hisss . . . sssss . . . plonk!
Fingers	Fingers to Look-Out. Come in, over.

Radio	Fizzle ... sizzle ... sputter ... spatter ... spitter ... whistle ... drone.
Fingers	Oi! Fingers to Look-Out. Are you there – keeping a look out? Just wait till I finish this job. If you're not doing your part of the deal then you won't get any of the loot. Now can you hear me?
Radio	Whine ... whistle ... whizzzzzzzzzzzzzzzzzzzzzzzzz.
Fingers	Look – I'm up to my waist down here in these drains. Cosher, can you hear me, over?
Radio	Ping ... whirrrrr ... spit ... rasp ... fizzzzzzzzzzzzzzzzz.
Fingers	Listen, Cosher. I'm nearly through. I'm still in the sewer but I'm nearly through. I'm right under the bank now. I'm about to do the final burst. That's why I need you. Is anyone about up there in the street? Will they hear the drill?
Radio	Rattle ... clatter ... tinkle ... tonkle ... jingle ... jangle.
Fingers	Fat lot of good you are as look-out if you're not tuned in on your walkie-talkie. That's the whole point of you being out there tonight – to keep watch outside the bank by the

	launderette. That's the whole point of using these blinking radio sets. So what are you playing at, Cosher?
Radio	Scratch . . . scramble . . . wheeze . . . zzzzzzzz.
Fingers	Right. One last try. I'll use our code names this time. Little John to Robin Hood, come in, over.
Radio	Pop . . . crackle . . . snap.
Fingers	Something is happening. It must be the channel. I'll change to channel 9. Now do you read me, Robin Hood?
Radio	Fizz . . . rattle . . . clatter . . . clung . . . dong . . . ping . . . kerplunk . . . croak . . . buzzzzzzzzzzzz.
	[*Meanwhile up in the street, P.C. Thumbs is out on the beat.*]
P.C.	Blimey! These blinking radio things are enough to scare the life out of anyone. One minute they're hissing away in your pocket and the next they're blasting away in your lug-hole. There's been nothing but snap, crackle and pop on here all night. It's worse than a bowl of Rice Crispies.
Radio	Tinkle . . . jingle . . . jangle.

P.C.	Blow this for a lark. Listen here. P.C. Thumbs to P.C. Washer, have you got into the building yet?
Radio	Scratch ... scramble ... screech ... sssssssssssssssssssssssssss.
P.C.	I'm in King Street on the corner outside the launderette, right next to the bank. In fact, I think I just saw an old friend of ours. It's a bit dark out here but it looked like old Cosher – with one of those walkie-talkie things. When he saw me, he ran off. Do you think he could be our suspect, over?
Radio	Hic ... burp ... cough ... splutter ... wheeze ... sh sh shshshshshshshshsh.
P.C.	P.C. Washer, are you there? P.C. Washer of the Drugs Squad, do you read me, over?
Radio	Grrrrrrrrrrrrrrrrrrrr.
P.C.	This is a waste of time if you ask me. So much for the tip-off that drugs are hidden in the flat above the launderette. I don't know why it has to be me who has to walk around on the look out while P.C. Washer gives the place the once over. It's cold and dark out here. Not a soul about – not a blooming soul.
Radio	Whine ... rumble ... squeak.
P.C.	Just me and this blinking radio. What a load

	of crackle and fuzz. Or as they say in the trade, *Splatter on the squawk box*. I just call it a blasted din.
Radio	Growl ... sp sp sps ch ch ch ch ch ch.
P.C.	See what I mean! This thing is blooming noisy tonight. It sounds like a drill. Even the path seems to be shaking.
Radio	Dr ... dr ... drrrrrrrrrrrrrrrrrrrr.
P.C.	I've never got the hang of these walkie-talkie things. I'd better get it right this time and use our proper call signs or handles or whatever we're called. Now, let me see. You push this button and say: Robin Red Breast to Johnny Jackdaw. Any sign of life?
Radio	Buzzz ... fizzz ... whizzzzz.
P.C.	Useless. That's what it is – useless. So much for all these gadgets. I'd much rather have my good old note book, handcuffs and truncheon instead of these new fangled radio sets. I'll try one last time.
Radio	Gurgle ... spurgle ... sfit sfit sfit.
P.C.	Well, if you're not going to answer, I'll move on. Maybe if I change the channel ... Let's try channel 9.
Radio	Scritch ... scritch ... scritch.

P.C.	Ah, this sounds more like it. I must be getting through. Are you in the flat above the launderette yet? Robin Red Breast to Johnny Jackdaw, are you there, over?
Fingers	Ah! I heard a voice. Little John to Robin Hood, are you there?
P.C.	Ah, a voice! Robin to John, do you read me?
Fingers	At last! John to Robin, come in, over.
P.C.	Robin to John.
Fingers	John to Robin.
P.C.	Ah, it's Washer.
Fingers	Ah, it's Cosher.
P.C.	Nothing happening out here – what about with you?
Fingers	I'm nearly through. Just one more shove and I'm there.
P.C.	How do you mean? Have you found anything!
Fingers	Not yet but I'm nearly through.
P.C.	Don't bank on it.
Fingers	What?
P.C.	I said, 'Don't bank on it'.

Fingers	Very funny.
P.C.	Why, what's the joke?
Fingers	I have done my sums you know. I've worked it all out to the last millimetre. It's all above my head now.
P.C.	So are you! This is all above my head. You're not making any sense.
Fingers	Only a few more minutes and I'll have my hands on it.
P.C.	So you think we're right? We'll get what we came for?
Fingers	Of course. Do you think I don't know what I'm doing?
P.C.	Any idea how much?
Fingers	Hundreds of pounds.
P.C.	Blimey! That's blooming heavy.
Fingers	Not really.
P.C.	It'll be worth millions.
Fingers	I don't think much of your maths!
P.C.	Is the sniffer dog on to anything yet?
Fingers	What are you going on about? Is the coast still clear?

P.C.	Clear as a bell. How much longer?
Fingers	Not long. I'll soon crack it.
P.C.	You what?
Fingers	With all this jelly. I'll soon crack the safe.
P.C.	Crack the safe? You mean, save the Crack!
Fingers	Eh? What's that?
P.C.	That's what it's called – Crack, drugs, dope.
Fingers	Don't you call me a dope. I'm the one with the brains.
P.C.	Make sure you find every scrap. Don't leave any behind.
Fingers	I'm only taking the used notes. Anyway, you keep your eyes open for blue-bottles.
P.C.	Eh?
Fingers	The fuzz.
P.C.	What do you mean?
Fingers	You know, the Sweeney, the Long Arm, the city kitty, the boys in blue.
P.C.	There's none of those out here. What about with you?
Fingers	Just rats.

P.C.	Rats? What's that noise? It's just like a drill. It's causing interference on the radio.
Fingers	What?
P.C.	Splatter on the squawk box.
Fingers	No, it's only my drill.
P.C.	What drill?
Fingers	I'm through the floor. It's pitch black in there. Just a couple of minutes and she'll blow.
P.C.	What do you mean? What are you going to do now?
Fingers	Blast it.
P.C.	Mind your language! It's pretty dull out here by this launderette. No sign of life.
Fingers	I'm going to use a saw now.
P.C.	Sshh, keep your voice down.
Fingers	Why? What do you mean?
P.C.	I thought I heard something just then.
Fingers	Is someone coming?
P.C.	I don't know.
Fingers	What did you hear?
P.C.	A sort of noise.

Fingers	What sort of a noise?
P.C.	A sort of sawing sort of noise. Then a different sort of noise.
Fingers	What sort of a different sort of noise?
P.C.	Well, a sort of a dragging sort of noise.
Fingers	What sort of like?
P.C.	Well, sort of like someone sort of dragging themself up through the floor.
Fingers	You what?
P.C.	With a clattering bag of tools.
Fingers	Don't be daft. You and your stupid jokes.
P.C.	But I'm not joking – I don't think.
Fingers	I nearly fell for that one.
P.C.	Sshhh. I'm sure there's someone there.
Fingers	Where?
P.C.	Inside.
Fingers	Inside where?
P.C.	Inside there.
Fingers	Yes, but inside where?
P.C.	There. Inside the launderette. By the tumble dryer.

Fingers	Don't be daft. They're shut at this time of night.
P.C.	I know. I can see that. It's pitch black inside. But I'm sure I heard something. I've got my nose pressed right up to the window.
Fingers	Sshh, sh!
P.C.	Eh?
Fingers	I just heard something.
P.C.	What?
Fingers	A creak.
P.C.	What sort of a creak?
Fingers	A squeaky freaky sort of creak.
P.C.	What like?
Fingers	Well – like the sound of a pane of glass being pushed.
P.C.	Can you see anything?
Fingers	Not a dicky bird. Oh hang on – crikey! It looks as though there's a patch on the window – where someone's been breathing. I'm not staying round here any longer. I'll light the fuse and then clear off.
P.C.	I can't see anything with my torch, either.

Fingers	Blimey. There's someone out there with a light.
P.C.	Wait a minute.
Fingers	What?
P.C.	I think I just saw something.
Fingers	What like?
P.C.	Like a flame – as if someone just struck a match inside the launderette.
Fingers	Then I'll come out in a minute. I won't be long. I've just lit the fuse and it will soon be over.
P.C.	I'll just have another look inside.
Fingers	Ah – I can't be sure but for a split second, I thought I saw a face at the window – sort of thing.
P.C.	What sort of like?
Fingers	It was horrible. There was just a couple of eyes staring inside at me.
P.C.	It can't be. There's no one out here and I can't see anyone inside. I'll have another peep but my breath keeps steaming up the glass.
Fingers	Ah! There it is again, with a horrible nose

	squashed up against the pane. Are you sure you can't see anything?
P.C.	It's pitch black in there.
Fingers	Oh no. Now the fuse has gone out. I'll have to strike another match.
P.C.	There it is again – a flame. Just a minute, did you say FUSE?
Fingers	Yeh – to the jelly.
P.C.	Jelly?
Fingers	Yep.
P.C.	What jelly?
Fingers	The jelly I packed round the door.
P.C.	What door?
Fingers	The door of the safe.
P.C.	What safe?
Fingers	You know very well what safe. The one I've just found in here – with a funny round door, a lot of funny buttons and what feels like a . . . ergh!
P.C.	What?
Fingers	I'm sitting in a puddle.
P.C.	Blimey, you must be frightened!

Fingers	No. Hold on, there's a little slot for money by the door. And a little drawer. How strange. I've never done a job like this before.
P.C.	A little drawer?
Fingers	It's full of powder.
P.C.	Is it drugs? Heroin?
Fingers	No, more like soap powder. Yuk!
P.C.	Now what?
Fingers	Yuk, I've just sat on a wet sock. It's just thirty seconds till she blows.
P.C.	Did you say sock?
Fingers	Yep.
P.C.	Did you say soap powder?
Fingers	Yep.
P.C.	Did you say a little slot for money?
Fingers	Yep.
P.C.	Do you know what I'm thinking?
Fingers	Oh blimey! Surely not. It can't be!
P.C.	I think it is.
Fingers	You don't mean I've made a blunder.

16

P.C.	I've only just put two and two together.
Fingers	I've made a bit of a bodge-up, haven't I?
P.C.	It does seem rather like it.
Fingers	I've dropped a clanger.
P.C.	A proper slip-up, mate, if you ask me.
Fingers	I've dropped a brick all right.
P.C.	Something of a bungle.
Fingers	I've made a bloomer.
P.C.	Exactly. So you're not in the flat upstairs at all, are you?
Fingers	Nope.
P.C.	And you're not P.C. Washer, code name Johnny Jackdaw, are you?
Fingers	Nope. Do you know what I'm also thinking?
P.C.	Nope.
Fingers	I'm not in the bank at all, am I?
P.C.	Nope.
Fingers	You're not Cosher, the look-out, code name Little John, are you?
P.C.	Nope.
Fingers	You know what I'm about to blow up, don't you?

P.C.	What?
	[*BOOM!*]
Fingers	An automatic washing machine front loader model delux!
P.C.	I thought as much.
Fingers	Full of underwear and soapy water.
P.C.	Then it looks like you've made a couple of errors, doesn't it?
Fingers	You could say a pair of bloomers!
P.C.	You what?
Fingers	Well, that's what I've got on my head. I'm covered with soggy clothes.
P.C.	Then I'm coming in after you.
Fingers	It's not my lucky day ... I'm smothered in shredded undies.
P.C.	I'll have to break open this door. I don't think we'll need these radios anymore. We can talk face to face now. My torch is all I need. [*Enters*] Ah, so there you are. Got you.
Fingers	Where are you?
P.C.	Take off that stupid thing over your head.
Fingers	You what?

P.C.	This is the police and you are under a vest!
Fingers	Oh knickers!
P.C.	No, it definitely looks like a vest to me. I must warn you that any thing you say may be taken down.
Fingers	Long-johns.
P.C.	I beg your pardon?
Fingers	I'm all tangled up in them. I'm all caught up in this underwear.
P.C.	Under where?
Fingers	Under here under the underwear.
P.C.	Then you are under arrest under there under the underwear, understand?
Fingers	Understood.
P.C.	I'll have to ask you to come with me to the station.
Fingers	Why? Don't you know the way on your own?
P.C.	The patrol car is just up the road. You're coming for a little spin with me.
Fingers	Well, that's just where you're wrong. Not a little spin and not with you! I'm going for a fast spin by myself – after a long rinse!
P.C.	What are you going on about? Are you going round the bend?

Fingers	No, but I soon will be – the 'U' bend. But I'm going round in this big machine first. [*Jumping inside the washing machine.*] With the door shut!
P.C.	Blimey – you can't do that! It's switched on. The door's locked! Come back. Speak to me. Say something. You'll kill yourself. Oh no, it's underway. You'll go underwater with the underwear!
Radio	Spurgle . . . glug . . . splatter . . . squawk.
P.C.	Ah, the radio! A signal is coming through on my speaker. Hello, can you hear me, over?
Fingers	Yes, and I shall go the same way that I came in – back down the sewer. You see, I'm much too clever for you!
P.C.	What do you mean?
Fingers	It's called the brain drain. I'm going out through the out-let pipe at the back of the washing machine!
P.C.	You mean. . . .
Fingers	Yes, I'll go through the hot wash and then get clean away!
P.C.	But if it goes into a fast spin you'll whoosh round like a catherine wheel. You'll disappear up your long-johns. You'll turn inside out. You'll turn over again and again.

Fingers	Well it's like I always say, 'One good turn deserves another!
P.C.	But just a minute... How come you're coming through on my radio? You left your walkie-talkie out here.
Fingers	Simple. It's all in the washing powder.
P.C.	Washing powder?
Fingers	You can't beat it for a clear radio signal.
P.C.	What on earth do you mean?
Fingers	ARIEL AUTOMATIC, of course! Over and out.

Glug
    glug
        glug
         glug.

The Thing from Above

2 parts:
Prof (an inventor), Radio (the voice of 'The Thing').

Scene	The Professor is fiddling with a giant radio machine in the kitchen.
Prof	It's me. Hello there!
Radio	Nnnnnnnnnnnnnnnnnnnnn.
Prof	I'm calling all of Space on this fine April morning. Every hour, on the hour.
Radio	Hummmmmmmmmmmmmmmmmmmmm.
Prof	It is ten hundred hours. This is Planet Earth. Are you there?
Radio	Zzzzzzzzzzzzzzzzzzzzz.
Prof	Can your hear me? Is there life up there? Come in, Outer Space. Do you read me, over?
Radio	Nnnnnnnnnnnnnnnnnnnnn.
Prof	Oh this is useless. I give up. Nothing. I'll

	never find out if there's life up there. I'll turn up the sound.
Radio	NNNNNNNNNOOOOOOOOOOOOOOOO.
Prof	Dead. For years I've been building my giant space dish to catch alien signals. For years I've been fixing it up to my computer. For years I've been tuning the Speak Machine. For years I've been fiddling with the radio mast up there on the roof of this block of flats. But all for nothing. What do I always get from the speaker?
Radio	Nnnnnnnnn ... hic ... hic ... nnnnnnn.
Prof	Every day since the first of January I have scanned the sky for signals. Every day for ninety days – and nothing. Yet one day I'm sure I'll contact life up there in the stars. I'll be famous. Everyone will know the great name of ... of ... oh blow, I can't remember it myself now!
Radio	Crackle ... nnnnnnn ... clunk ... click ... nnnnnnn ... plip ...
Prof	Well fancy that! For a split second I thought ...
Radio	Shshshshshshshshshsh ... groink ... groink ... groink.

Prof	A pulse on the air waves! This is it! The moment I've longed for!
Radio	Sssssssssss ... ffffffffffff ... zzzzzzzzzz ... twang ... oops!
Prof	Amazing! I'm getting all in a tiz. I must turn this switch here, press that there, pull this lever, slide that along there, twiddle this button, double the power, treble the out-put, adjust the R.P.M. and put another coin in the meter!
Radio	O11! O11! O11! Eh!
Prof	Yes! Something's there! At last. Go ahead, speak. This is Planet Earth. I'm hearing you loud and clear.
Radio	O11. O11 eh!
Prof	But what does it mean? I must switch on my Speak Machine. It will turn the sound waves into English. It's taken me years on the computer to get this right. Years of sleepless nights. Years of stress, panic and worry.
Radio	O11 eh! O11 eh!
Prof	Keep talking. Don't go away. I'll just program the computer.
Radio	O11 eh! O11 eh!

Prof	It sounds like Spanish to me. Let me feed it into my computer word bank.
Radio	011 eh. Yad doog. Yad doog.
Prof	Yad doog? Are you Russian? Ah, of course, I forgot the floppy disk.
Radio	Yad doog. Yad doog.
Prof	Just hold on. I'm typing it all in. Yad doog.
Radio	KO.
Prof	KO? Oh yes! KO comes out as OK. So that's it! It's just back to front. YAD DOOG is GOOD DAY and OLL EH is HELLO! I've done it! I've cracked it. I've made contact. Well fancy that!
Radio	How do you od?
Prof	How do you od? What does it mean by that? Oh, I see – the keyboard has jammed. I'll press ERROR and ESCAPE. That should do the trick. Now press SPACE and RETURN.
Radio	Try SHIFT and BREAK.
Prof	Well I never! Who on earth are you? Oh, of course, that's the whole point – you're not on earth at all, are you? What is your name?
Radio	Thing.
Prof	Thing?

Radio	That is my name. I am Thing. I am E.T.'s uncle.
Prof	E.T.? Who is E.T.?
Radio	My nephew.
Prof	Well fancy that! So it must be his trousers I've got on! It says E.T. on the label. I always thought that meant 'Extra Tight'. But where are you speaking from?
Radio	Up here.
Prof	Where's that for heaven's sake?
Radio	That's right – we're right next door to heaven. If you go to heaven, turn left at the black hole and we're the next cosmos on the right. It's great here – out of this world.
Prof	So what is your planet called.
Radio	Planet Cuboid.
Prof	Never heard of it.
Radio	We're millions of light years away from earth. We're in the Sugar Lump Galaxy.
Prof	Sugar lump? What's that?
Radio	It's where all the planets have six flat edges and are made of icing and toffee.
Prof	Really? But what's it like?

Radio	It's fine as long as it doesn't get too hot.
Prof	Why's that?
Radio	Everything gets stuck. It all gets clogged up – all sticky and gummed up.
Prof	Yes, I have that trouble too. With my new hair gel.
Radio	In winter it's like one big choc-ice. Sugar drifts down from the sky and we get covered in it.
Prof	So your planet is like a giant toffee?
Radio	Exactly. In fact there are two.
Prof	Two planets the same?
Radio	Better known as The Twix.
Prof	Amazing.
Radio	After all, you've heard of the other chocolate planets, I'm sure.
Prof	No, I can't say I have.
Radio	Well, there's Mars, Milky Way, Galaxy ... and now there's Planet Twix.
Prof	But doesn't it rot your teeth?
Radio	Teeth? What are teeth?
Prof	They're things that you need at meal times and they're not much fun when you get old.

Radio	Oh yes, we have those. We call them Macdonalds.
Prof	Gosh. Let me write all this down. I'll put it all in my book. No one will believe all this. Are you still hearing me loud and clear?
Radio	You bet, Earthling. Real cool.
Prof	What sort of radio are you using to pick up my signal?
Radio	A 'Walk-thing'.
Prof	A 'Walk-thing?' What's that?
Radio	You've heard of a 'Walkman' for people so this is a 'Walk-thing' for Things.
Prof	Well fancy that! I'm over the moon!
Radio	But you just said you were on Earth – so how can you be over the moon at the same time? Are you in a super M.G. turbo-jet star-ship G.T.S. twin carb with atom rocket boosters!
Prof	Not really, I'm sitting by the sink in my council flat. But listen, I'm dying to ask you so many questions. Let me switch on the tape. Now then, what are you like? How do you think? Sorry about all these questions but all this has gone to my head.
Radio	Head? What is 'head'?

Prof	You use it to think with.
Radio	Oh, those.
Prof	Those? You mean you've got more than one?
Radio	Of course. I've got ten of them.
Prof	Just fancy that! You must be very clever. Just think of it.
Radio	Oh I do – ten times at once.
Prof	But just think – ten heads! All those brains. All that mind power!
Radio	Yes, but I got drunk last week.
Prof	What's that got to do with it?
Radio	Have you ever had ten hang-overs all at once?
Prof	But ten heads – you must be so clever.
Radio	Oh yes, I can be when I put my heads together.
Prof	Then say something really clever now.
Radio	You really want me to?
Prof	Oh yes. Something mind-blowing. Something out of this world.
Radio	Are you ready then?
Prof	Yes. Go on, impress me.

Radio	G.C.S.E.
Prof	Well, fancy that!
Radio	You see, I'm pretty good with letters.
Prof	Same here, I used to be a postman. But say some more.
Radio	My U.F.O. flew over the U.S.A. at great M.P.H. and R.P.M. The F.B.I. sent an S.O.S. to H.Q. but by then I was over the U.K. being chased by the R.A.F. and watched by a D.J. on B.B.C. T.V. So I stopped off on my B.M.X. in the U.S.S.R. for P.G. Tips and a W.C.
Prof	W.C.?
Radio	Winter Coat.
Prof	Well, fancy that – having ten brains at once!
Radio	That's the problem. They never want to do the same thing all at once. If one brain needs to go to sleep, you can bet that another one wants to watch 'East Enders' and you spend all night having a row with yourself! It also costs a fortune at the hairdressers.
Prof	So you have hair! What colour?
Radio	Purplow.
Prof	Purplow? Never heard of it.

Radio	You don't get it on Earth. It's a colour you don't get.
Prof	How do you know that? Can you see us from your planet?
Radio	No, but I've often been there.
Prof	Well, fancy that! You've really set foot on our planet? You've seen for yourself real human life – real people?
Radio	Oh no. I stayed at Butlins.
Prof	Well, I'll be dashed! But why did you come to Earth?
Radio	I was just passing. I needed fuel for the rocket – one million litres.
Prof	Where on earth did you get that much?
Radio	Some little platform thing in the middle of lots of blue wet stuff.
Prof	The North Sea!
Radio	But there was a problem.
Prof	Didn't they want to sell you any petrol?
Radio	That wasn't the problem – it was the blinking sherry glasses with every six litres! By the way ... by the way ... by the way...

Prof	Yes? What is it?
Radio	By the way . . . by the way . . . by the way . . .
Prof	Oh crumbs! Something's stuck. There's smoke coming from the disk drive.
Radio	I'm having trouble with the signal. There's background fizz – or as we call it up here. 'Splatter on the Squawk Box'.
Prof	Turn your squelch button.
Radio	I beg your pardon?
Prof	You need to tune your set.
Radio	TWANG! Oops, a wire has come loose.
Prof	Where abouts?
Radio	Well, on the side. By the switch sort of thing.
Prof	Tell me some more and I can tell you how to fix it.
Radio	Well – it's on the thing-a-me-jig by the what's-its-name. It's under the doo-dah on top of the what-not in the oo-jah thing-a-me-bob.
Prof	Oh dear. Well what about it?
Radio	It's come off.

Prof	I'm not too clear what you mean. Could you put it any clearer?
Radio	Of course. It's the micro plug by the electra prong, under the safety-catch, beside the mega-sprocket, on top of the curly pin in the ultra-bracket, on the whirly clip fixed in the sonic dimmer grip switch.
Prof	Oh, is that all? Then all you need is a micro thin coating of poly fixing super cream of hyper-grip mega stress.
Radio	Eh?
Prof	Glue.
Radio	Right. Well, I'll sign off for now, then – or as we say up here, 'I'll back off and bow out!'
Prof	Oh no – don't do that. I've still got so many questions. Just cut down the power for a few minutes so you can fix it. Understand?
	[*The cut in power makes the answers come back a bit late!*]
Radio	Nnnnnnnnnnnnnnnnnnnnnn.
Prof	Oh no. There's no answer. What shall I do now?
Radio	Yes.

Prof	I beg your pardon? Why did you say 'Yes'?
Radio	Nnnnnnnnnnnnnnn.
Prof	I don't get this. Where are you, thing?
Radio	Because you asked me if I understood and I do.
Prof	Eh? Oh, I see now! The power is cut, so your answers take a bit longer to reach my set. Let me try again with my questions. Are you ready?
Radio	Nnnnnnnnnnnnnnn.
Prof	Of course, I forgot! I must wait a bit longer for the answer. What is the weather like where you are?
Radio	Yes.
Prof	Oh, that must have been the answer to my first question! I mustn't forget to allow ten seconds for the answer. Now tell me about your wife. What is she like?
Radio	Hot and steamy and only just stopped spitting. The wind is still bad.
Prof	Blimey! Oh, I see what you mean! I need to wait a bit. Have you got any cars and what are they like?
Radio	Very pretty with green hair, frilly clothes and sexy.

Prof	Well, fancy that! Do you have any children?
Radio	Yes. They're silver, made of iron, they can fly upside down and they run on micro chips. I'm thinking of melting them down for scrap.
Prof	Just fancy! Do you have a favourite food?
Radio	Yes. Baby boys.
Prof	This is confusing! Do you mind if I ask you which of your children take after you?
Radio	Yes. Rhubarb.
Prof	Sorry I asked! Oh, I see what you mean now. What about your best films or videos?
Radio	Only the naughty ones.
Prof	Who is your leader, your Prime Minister, your wise ruler?
Radio	Donald Duck.
Prof	Amazing. I only hope my machine can make sense of this. I think it might be better if you turned up the power again so I can answer your questions. If you don't put the power up, I'll be answering your questions before you've asked them!
Radio	But I don't need to ask you any questions.
Prof	Why's that? Aren't you interested in us?

Radio	I already know.
Prof	What do you mean by that?
Radio	I've been watching you.
Prof	Watching me? But you don't know where I live.
Radio	Oh yes I do. Number 326 The Flats. You've got spiky hair and glasses. You've got a cat called Smutty, you had two kippers for breakfast, the dustman calls on Tuesdays – and you listen to UB40 on the hi-fi.
Prof	Well fancy that! How do you know all this? How can you see me? Have you been spying on me through a telescope?
Radio	I don't have to. I can hear you. We can all hear you.
Prof	You mean you've actually heard me calling you every morning?
Radio	Loud and clear.
Prof	For the past ninety days?
Radio	Clear as a bell.
Prof	For hours on end?
Radio	Hour after hour after hour.
Prof	Till I'm at my wits' end?

Radio	Till you go bananas.
Prof	Yet you never answered until now?
Radio	Correct.
Prof	But I could have gone mad!
Radio	So could we. In fact some of us have.
Prof	But why have you left it so long to answer?
Radio	Do you really want to know?
Prof	Yes. Why didn't you speak till this morning?
Radio	I couldn't.
Prof	What do you mean – you couldn't?
Radio	It wouldn't have been right.
Prof	I don't understand.
Radio	I was waiting.
Prof	Waiting? Waiting for what?
Radio	This very morning.
Prof	Why? What's so special about today?
Radio	Look at the calendar.
Prof	Yes, but what's so special?
Radio	The time of year.
Prof	What's that got to do with it?

Radio	It's just right.
Prof	Oh, you mean something to do with our orbit?
Radio	Not really.
Prof	Or the position of the stars or moon?
Radio	No.
Prof	Or the axis of the Earth.
Radio	Not quite.
Prof	Then what? Tell me what.
Radio	The month.
Prof	So what? What's special about the start of the fourth month?
Radio	Today's the day.
Prof	The day for what?
Radio	To strike back.
Prof	How do you mean?
Radio	It's dragged on now for too long.
Prof	What? Tell me.
Radio	Day after day.
Prof	You're not making sense.
Radio	Night after night.

Prof	You're walking in tiddles ... er talking in widdles ... I mean talking in riddles.
Radio	Hour after hour you've kept me awake with your bleeps.
Prof	Surely not.
Radio	Those bleeps and splatters. Just as I'm dropping off, your voice comes blasting through. 'Is anybody there – it's me!' Again and again.
Prof	Yes, I know.
Radio	The din on my radio, the constant crackle and fizz all through my head. Well, it's sending me bonkers, do you hear?
Prof	But why didn't you say something before? Just tell me why you didn't beam down your message from Sugar Lump Galaxy. From Planet Cuboid.
Radio	It had to be done properly.
Prof	All I wanted to know was if there was life up there.
Radio	Well, now you know there is.
Prof	I won't bother you again. Now I can go away and write my book.
Radio	Good.

Prof	Now I will be famous all round the world. I have made contact.
Radio	You've done that all right.
Prof	Everyone will know who I am.
Radio	Yes. A stark raving loony.
Prof	I'll tell the whole world about you.
Radio	That's a joke!
Prof	The Thing from Outer Space.
Radio	They'll never believe you.
Prof	Of course they will. You've told me and it's all on tape.
Radio	Amazing!
Prof	I'll tell the newspapers who you are and where you live. They'll all want to know about us both – I'll be rich. They'll all want to hear this tape.
Radio	Then they'd better listen to the next bit.
Prof	I'll be known as the professor who spoke to the power above ... I've made contact with that Life Force in the sky ...
Radio	I hardly think so, mate. After all, I'm only the bloke in the flat upstairs. April Fool! Over and out!!